Anxiety

A Pragmatic Handbook For Women. A Comprehensive Handbook On Ceasing Excessive Pondering On Past Events And Anxiety Regarding Future Matters With An Emphasis On Emotional Well-Being

Darryl Roth

TABLE OF CONTENT

Introduction 1

Approaches Towards Managing Anxiety And Disrupting Negative Self-Dialogue 13

What Is The Impact Of Anxiety On Interpersonal Relationships? 43

Methods For Releasing Inner Trust 55

"What Makes Creative Hopelessness Such A Potent Tool? 88

Gaining Insight Into The Kinetics Of Human Physiology 98

The Significance Of Adverse Thinking 113

Reveal The Underlying Factors That Elicit Stress 117

Positive Emotions 126

Managing Panic Attacks And Anxiety 136

Body Language And How You Appear 165

Introduction

This publication offers well-established methods and approaches for enhancing one's well-being and cultivating a sense of contentment by means of an array of effortlessly executed breathing exercises.

In an environment characterized by rapidity, one perceives the necessity of adapting in order to thrive, even if one's inclination is to prioritize a more leisurely approach to tasks. When such circumstances arise, it is inherent that one experiences heightened levels of stress, which may consequently lead to the development of more severe conditions.

The respiratory techniques that will be acquired from the contents of this literary work will aid individuals in effectively managing the persistent occurrences of alterations in their surroundings.

This book also comprises methods to facilitate relaxation and overcome feelings of anxiety and depression. In addition to that, you will acquire knowledge regarding proper breathing techniques in order to optimize your focus, increase vitality, stabilize your emotions, and alleviate persistent discomfort.

I trust that this book will provide you with the solutions you have been seeking.

Thank you once again for acquiring this book. I genuinely hope that you find it enjoyable and enriching.

6 Strategies for Enhancing Happiness

The concept of happiness is one that elicits considerable debate within the realm of social science. Happiness has been subject to various interpretations across academic disciplines, ranging from philosophy to psychology. Notwithstanding its intricacy, each individual has encountered happiness at some juncture. It elicits a sense of jubilation that brings forth a positive emotional response. Consequently, we desire to hold on to that sensation.

However, the global landscape continues to grow increasingly intricate. There has been a shift in our lifestyle. Happiness has become elusive. Life appears challenging, as it is commonly perceived. The attainment of happiness has transformed into a luxury accessible only to a privileged few.

However, the reality is precisely contrary. Pursuing happiness is not an advisable course of action. Instead, it is something that can be selected. Indeed, several experts in the field of happiness posit that one's happiness is ultimately determined by the choices they make. And this can be achieved through the selection of appropriate thoughts - specifically, those that are optimistic in nature. And by avoiding the negative imaginations.

Consequently, the matter at hand is not determining the factors that bring us happiness, but rather evaluating our own capacity and readiness to embrace happiness. The paramount understanding to be gleaned from this matter is that an existence of contentment can be attained by all individuals. Provided that he or she elects to embrace contentment.

Presently, I will delve into a few of the elixirs of happiness. If one comprehends and implements these principles in their life, they will attain a heightened state of happiness.

1. A contented life consists of an accumulation of moments of joy.

That\\\'s right. To experience happiness, one must make the conscious decision to embrace happiness and refrain from harboring any concerns or apprehensions. Undoubtedly, life perpetually presents challenges. You consistently strive to meet your daily necessities. And that necessitates a significant amount of exertion. If successful, you will experience a positive sensation. Otherwise, you will experience a sense of resentment and an increase in anxiety. However, adopting an optimistic perspective will reveal ample justification for experiencing positivity.

In situations where circumstances are unfavorable, the optimal course of action is to evaluate the extent to which you possess influence or authority over said circumstances. Engaging in a thorough assessment greatly assists in the development and refinement of one's emotional well-being. As one must take into account that without exerting influence over the aspects that went awry, there exists no justification for experiencing sorrow.

Experiencing negative emotions in response to a challenging situation is within the realm of expectations, however, it is imperative that you liberate yourself from the grip of said emotions. It is imperative to engage in the cultivation of one's mindset in order to attain a state of happiness.

Happiness does not solely depend on favorable life circumstances, but rather on maintaining a positive perspective towards life's events. Sadness cannot solve chaos. One cannot mend what is fractured by confining oneself within the confines of pessimistic emotions. You are merely burdening yourself with significant responsibilities. Therefore, seek out factors that contribute to your overall sense of happiness.

2. A contented existence is one that is characterized by gratitude.

Hatred diminishes one's proclivity for experiencing happiness. The commencement of happiness occurs through the cultivation of gratitude. Express gratitude for all that has transpired in your life. For all the blessings you possess - a wonderful family, cherished friends, and meaningful relationships. By adopting this approach, you are able to relinquish negativity and nurture a sense of contentment within yourself.

3. A joyous existence revolves around the act of pardoning.

Residing in a state of frustration and animosity will restrict you to the realm of negative emotions, specifically sadness. Adverse emotions can have a pronounced effect on your psychological well-being. Hence, individuals who harbor grudges and resentment are at a greater likelihood of developing health complications. Experiencing feelings of sadness and anger is a natural response, however, it is imperative to actively work towards releasing oneself from the grip of these emotions expeditiously. And commence granting forgiveness to those individuals who have committed wrongdoings against you. While this statement may appear more simplistic, it is in fact more complex than it seems. It necessitates a sincere dedication.

To implement forgiveness effectively, it is necessary to empathize with the individuals who have committed the wrongdoing. Make an effort to comprehend the reasons behind their actions towards you. This method has the potential to aid in the resolution of your unbalanced evaluation. Strive for altruism as a means of transcending animosity. Exhibit a readiness to relinquish and let go of personal commitments for the betterment of others. And you will experience an increased level of happiness like never before!

4. "Happiness is a state of mind filled with pure joy.

Joy is an outcome resulting from a mindset that embraces positivity. If you have happy evaluation about your life, you will be happy. Hence, it is impossible to achieve happiness through the harboring of pessimistic thoughts.

In the event that you become aware of your inclination towards negativity, endeavor to redirect your cognitive processes. Prompt a critical examination of that notion by inquiring about its underlying rationale. Is it imperative to experience feelings of sadness or frustration? This will enable you to refrain from developing pessimistic thoughts.

What is the significance of vigilance towards negative thoughts? Indeed, the human mind functions akin to a magnetic force. It attracts the like. Positive thinking generates positive outcomes. If one experiences contentment, they tend to draw likeminded individuals who exhibit a similar state of happiness. However, in the event that you experience anger, you will inevitably attract individuals who possess a similar disposition of negativity and anger. This denotes what is commonly referred to as The Law of Attraction. The principle of the law of attraction further posits that experiencing contentment significantly contributes to the accomplishment of one's life objectives.

5. One's level of happiness is not contingent upon financial wealth.

Money can contribute to one's happiness to a certain extent. Undoubtedly, financial wealth is not the sole determinant of one's sense of happiness. The most significant aspect lies in the bond between individuals. It entails potential associations with individuals encompassing one's parents, neighbors, siblings, co-workers, and others of similar nature. Not money. This is the underlying cause behind the ability of individuals in underdeveloped nations to experience contentment despite their limited financial means. In order to experience feelings of happiness, it is essential to place significance on the interpersonal connections one cultivates. Express gratitude and value the precious moments spent with your dear ones.

6. A contented life is contingent upon fostering strong social ties.

Humans are social animals. It is imperative that you do not reside in isolation. You are interconnected within the broader tapestry of existence. And the good thing about this is that being connected with others make you happy. The potential to forge meaningful friendships is vast. An increase in the number of friends will enhance one's level of happiness.

Consequently, establish strong and positive connections with individuals. Value the moments you have in your life with your loved ones. In my perspective, the epitome of life's purpose is attaining happiness. Individuals who reside in an environment characterized by animosity and discontent are those who fail to comprehend the true essence of their being.

In existence, one's possessions are not measured by their quantity, but rather by the appreciation bestowed upon them. This constitutes the pathway to achieving happiness.

Approaches Towards Managing Anxiety And Disrupting Negative Self-Dialogue

The process of reconfiguring your cognitive patterns, enhancing your resilience against anxiety, and cultivating a deeper sense of self-assurance entails modifying your thought processes, perspectives, and behavioral reactions. If you are able to achieve proficiency in this area, you will be making significant progress. However, the primary objective of this book is to provide you with practical knowledge that will prove valuable in facilitating your journey. Please consider reviewing these strategies designed to combat anxiety and ascertain if any of them resonate with you.

✲ ✲ ✲

The approach of visual inspection, observation, and tactile perception: When individuals begin to experience anxiety, they tend to engage in a variety of negative cognitive processes. This situation is unfavorable, as the presence of negative thoughts can lead to a perpetuation of further negative thoughts, potentially exacerbating the severity of anxiety. In order to assist you in breaking this recurring pattern, you may employ the technique known as the observe, perceive, and experience approach. It is essential to engage in a practice where, upon experiencing feelings of anxiety, one takes a moment to pause, observe the surrounding environment, and identify a minimum of six visible objects. Additionally, it is recommended to identify six discernible sounds and engage in physical movements across various body parts to heighten sensory awareness. (Instances of this could involve making movements with your fingers or exerting pressure on your toes.)

✱ ✱ ✱

Exercise caution in moderating your consumption of caffeine and alcohol: It is worth noting that caffeine induces a state of restlessness by triggering the fight or flight response. Alcohol exerts an influence on neurotransmitters such as serotonin, which is known for its role in eliciting positive emotions. This will contribute to an individual exhibiting a heightened susceptibility to anxiety or exacerbating their pre-existing anxiety. Caffeine possesses the capacity to stimulate heightened cognitive activity, owing to its intended purpose of providing an energizing effect. Although this approach may prove effective for certain individuals, it is important to acknowledge that it can induce heightened mental activity, resulting in accelerated respiration and compromised cognitive judgment for others.

Avoid excessive rumination: Individuals grappling with anxiety and diminished self-assurance often place an undue amount of importance on the opinions of others. Additionally, they have a tendency to overly contemplate matters in a general sense. Individuals who experience anxiety often engage in the process of dwelling on adverse consequences. They will conjure negative outcomes or envisage mishaps occurring. This is the juncture at which uncertainty and concern manifest. Cease the excessive rumination and direct your attention towards the current moment. Engaging in this behavior causes an individual to lose their rationality. Your anxiety shall diminish or, at the very least, undergo a significant reduction. If one is inclined to engage in excessive contemplation, it would be more beneficial to direct one's thoughts towards the reasons why a situation is likely to unfold favorably, rather than dwelling on potential negative outcomes.

❋ ❋ ❋

Proactively pursue circumstances where you can confront anxiety directly: It is noteworthy that a minority of individuals may not possess familiarity with the anime series 'Dragon Ball Z'; nevertheless, the character 'Goku' typically proactively approaches proficient martial artists and engages in sparring sessions as a means of evaluating their strength. Irrespective of the outcome, the objective is for him to encounter formidable opponents, thereby nurturing his skills and bolstering his overall capabilities. Occasionally, when dealing with anxiety, one must actively pursue and confront it directly. You may commence with modest beginnings, yet as you accumulate an increasing number of triumphs within your repertoire, you shall gradually perceive that many of the sources of your anxiety were the very entities to which you attributed excessive significance.

Eliminate negative self-dialogue: Despite its apparent simplicity, it is rather astonishing to observe the number of individuals who exacerbate their anxiety through the indulgence of pessimistic internal narratives. In accordance with the proverbial wisdom, "what you focus on expands," the act of indulging in negative self-dialogue has the potential to significantly amplify the significance of a given matter beyond its actual magnitude. Rather, direct your attention towards self-dialogue that is empowering. Consider positive aspects, offer self-inspiring affirmations. Kindly contemplate the creation of potent affirmations that can be utilized to undermine the influence of anxiety. You might find it astonishing the efficacy of this approach when executed correctly.

Acquire an understanding of the stimuli that provoke anxiety and explore effective strategies to mitigate its impact: Anxiety invariably arises in response to specific triggers, and through a thorough evaluation of these instances, one can discern their root causes. For instance, an individual may experience heightened emotional reactions upon hearing boisterous laughter from a nearby group (potentially directed towards oneself). This phenomenon is attributed to cognitive processes involving the perception and interpretation of the situation. Another individual may experience emotional distress when confronted with the concept of numerous individuals focusing their attention on them simultaneously. Anxiety triggers are typically commonplace, yet by acquiring the ability to mitigate the impact of such triggers, one can effectively manage anxiety. Contemplate the underlying reasons behind the elicitation of these triggers, which consequently result in the emergence of negative emotions. What is the source of your apprehension? In accordance with the discourse previously expounded in an antecedent chapter, it was highlighted that a majority of individuals exhibit a greater apprehension towards psychological anguish as opposed to physical affliction. The aforementioned methods are straightforward and can be implemented immediately. And they were deliberately created with a focus on customizable features. We kindly request you to allocate some time to contemplate at least one of these options. Individuals vary in terms of their characteristics and preferences, hence necessitating the recognition that a particular approach may yield more favorable results for certain individuals as opposed to others. Recall the previous statement made, that doubt and worry serve as a formidable combination, inducing feelings of anxiety. By directing your attention towards managing these factors through effective rationalization, you will be able to conquer these adverse emotions. When one successfully manages to overcome these obstacles, they effectively conquer anxiety.

Is Your Child Affected by Social Anxiety Disorder?

In order for your child to receive a diagnosis of social anxiety disorder, it is necessary for them to exhibit a significant level of apprehension regarding potential humiliation during social engagements, to the extent that their ability to perform daily activities is substantially hindered. The individual will likely make an earnest effort to avoid circumstances or occasions that they perceive as being closely connected to their anxiety, so as to prevent experiencing any potential ramifications. It can be observed that your child may exhibit a reluctance to attend the birthday party of their closest companion, or demonstrate an aversion to engaging with peers beyond the immediate family circle. Should your child be diagnosed with social anxiety disorder, they may endure an exceptionally intense level of anxiety, giving rise to various indications of social anxiety, such as excessive perspiration, trembling, and difficulty breathing. Children of a younger age may exhibit instances of throwing tantrums and shedding tears as they express episodes of social anxiety. One alternative phrasing in a formal tone could be: "Another factor that can induce anxiety in a child is the perception that they will face adverse scrutiny or potential punitive measures as a consequence of displaying signs of anxiety."

In order for your child to qualify for a diagnosis of social anxiety disorder, it is necessary that his or her anxiety is evident specifically in the company of peers, rather than solely when in the presence of adults. Furthermore, this anxious reaction must have been enduring for a duration of at least six months. The sole individual capable of definitively and appropriately diagnosing your child with social anxiety disorder is a duly certified healthcare practitioner. Nevertheless, it is important to note that instances of misdiagnosis do occur. Each child experiences a degree of social anxiety as a natural part of their developmental process. Correct diagnosis is only possible in cases of severe persistence.

It is conceivable that your child, should they possess it, may potentially negate their experience of anxiety in social circumstances or minimize the symptoms associated with it due to apprehension of negative evaluation, scrutiny, or potential embarrassment. Upon occurrence of this phenomenon, the diagnostic healthcare practitioner will be required to engage in discussions with you, the parents, as well as the nannies and teachers to gain comprehensive insights into the observable symptoms and, subsequently, undertake a precise assessment and diagnosis thereof.

Treatments

Do not despair if your child receives an official diagnosis of social anxiety disorder. The reason for this is that social anxiety is a highly manageable condition, which exhibits notable response to behavioral therapy, thereby reducing the necessity for prescribing medication at such a tender age. The objective of therapy is to assist your child in altering their cognitive processes as the primary means of effectively dealing with or handling social anxiety. Even in cases where children are undergoing a combination regimen of behavioral therapy and prescription medication, it has been observed that behavioral therapy yields significant effectiveness, leading to reduced reliance on medication over time.

Please be mindful that the prompt identification of an issue will enhance the likelihood of its successful resolution. Individuals who only receive a diagnosis of Seasonal Affective Disorder (SAD) during adulthood encounter significantly greater challenges compared to those who receive the diagnosis during their childhood years. Young individuals are less likely to develop deep-rooted negative thought patterns, and even if they do, they tend to be more receptive to interventions aimed at breaking those patterns in comparison to their older counterparts. Indeed, the task of instilling new knowledge or skills in an elder canine proves to be more challenging than imparting the same to a young and inexperienced puppy.

Behavioral Therapy

Through the utilization of behavioral therapy, it is highly likely that a certified therapist will commence treatment by employing cognitive behavioral therapy (CBT) to enhance your child's coping mechanisms and social aptitude in circumstances that may incite their social anxiety. Cognitive Behavioral Therapy (CBT) enables children to discover their ability to effectively regulate and exert control over their unfavorable reactions and anxiety. Therapy imparts the tools and techniques for individuals to conquer their fears and by altering their anxious cognitive patterns.

Another form of therapy, known as exposure therapy, entails systematically and progressively exposing individuals to anxiety-provoking situations under highly controlled circumstances. The primary objective is to desensitize them to these situations over time, ultimately decreasing or mitigating their anxiety responses.

Prescription Medicines

If behavioral therapy proves insufficient, physicians have the option to prescribe medication as a means to mitigate your child's social anxiety. In numerous instances, prescription medications enhance the efficacy of behavioral therapy, as previously stated, and typically these are administered for a limited duration.

Similar to adult social anxiety, it is possible that your child's healthcare provider might recommend the use of selective serotonin reuptake inhibitors (SSRI) or beta blockers. These medications have the potential to alleviate your child's anxiety by suppressing their fearful reactions to social anxiety-inducing situations, while also minimizing the physical manifestations of anxiety such as excessive perspiration, palpitations, and breathlessness.

What Is The Impact Of Anxiety On Interpersonal Relationships?

No experience compares to the joy and fulfillment brought by a flourishing and harmonious relationship. The persistent sensation of exhilaration akin to intoxication resembles the euphoria induced by a potent substance, causing one's concerns and responsibilities to dissolve into insignificance. Humans are inclined to seek emotional bonds with one another. Establishing and nurturing wholesome relationships contribute to the enrichment and meaning of one's existence. It is not surprising that individuals go to great lengths to find a companion with whom they can share their life.

Upon receiving favorable or potentially unfavorable information, individuals tend to have an innate inclination to confide in a trusted companion. The presence of another individual to commemorate positive news and support us during challenging times undeniably amplifies our joy and mitigates the hardship we encounter. The correlation between the quality of interpersonal relationships and the overall quality of life experienced by individuals is unsurprising.

In order to establish a genuine emotional connection with an individual, one must be prepared to exhibit vulnerability and possess the self-assurance to expose their vulnerabilities to their significant other. Regrettably, for the majority of individuals afflicted with anxiety, this is frequently beyond their capacity. Establishing and nurturing relationships, even under optimal circumstances, necessitates substantial effort and dedication. When anxiety is introduced into the equation alongside common trials, the complexity of relationships is significantly amplified.

We have thoroughly examined the role that fear plays as a primary catalyst for the onset of hysteria. So, in what way can an individual who already experiences fear of abandonment manage to develop a sense of ease and vulnerability in order to establish emotional intimacy with their significant other? Clearly, they will not. In the majority of instances, individuals will assume a facade as a means of safeguarding themselves from emotional harm.

Anxiety has multifaceted implications on one's relationship, inducing changes in both emotional and behavioral responses. Some individuals may develop excessive dependence on their partners due to their persistent need for reassurance. Additional individuals exhibit tendencies of isolation and emotional detachment as a means of safeguarding themselves against potential emotional harm. Some individuals may choose to eschew romantic relationships altogether and opt for social isolation, as they are unwilling to traverse the realm of uncertainty surrounding the potential outcomes of such partnerships.

Areas of Concern

We have extensively discussed the various manifestations of anxiety. I am also interested in learning about different facets of your life and their connection to your anxiety. Anxiety frequently diminishes the overall quality of life. Occasionally, life circumstances can elicit or exacerbate feelings of anxiety, such as engaging in demanding professional endeavors or navigating the process of marital dissolution. The prevailing circumstances of your existence serve as the backdrop for the persistent presence of anxiety, thus necessitating our thorough contemplation.

Allow us to pause briefly and assess every facet of your life at this moment. I kindly request that you engage in introspection regarding your current progress, identify areas in which you believe enhancement is needed, and explore the impact of anxiety on your well-being.

Social Interactions

Anne is cognizant of the fact that her anxiety is giving rise to difficulties within her marital relationship and affecting her friendships. Her persistent requirement for affirmation with regards to even the most minuscule matters has alienated individuals from her, including those in her inner circle. She muses, 'I simply long for the opportunity to recline and unwind, much like the rest of the individuals.' Subsequently, they would perceive that I still retain a measure of enjoyment

Anxiety has the potential to adversely affect interpersonal connections, while simultaneously, issues within relationships can amplify one's experience of anxiety. Social anxiety can lead to a sense of seclusion and alienation. It poses difficulties in cultivating new interpersonal relationships. Panic attacks may induce a sense of shame in individuals. Frequently, the social disapproval associated with experiencing anxiety can exert a comparable level of hardship to the actual symptoms of anxiety. Furthermore, issues within interpersonal connections can exacerbate symptoms of anxiety. Challenging circumstances such as navigating through a divorce can engender additional concerns that compound the existing load, rendering it arduous to manage.

Consider your personal circumstances. In what manner has anxiety influenced your interpersonal connections? In consideration of the individuals that comprise your social circle, you may contemplate your familial relations, companions, significant other, or offspring, thereby influencing your thoughts. Do you have a trusted friend or advisor that you confide in? Are you currently experiencing any alterations or changes in your interpersonal connections? Do you encounter difficulty in establishing new friendships? Kindly document your reflections within the designated area provided.

Education and Work

Anne was aware that her anxiety was impeding her job performance. Furthermore, besides her persistent tendency to scrutinize her work excessively, she had additionally been disregarded for a promotion due to the perception that she exhibited excessive anxiety and caused discomfort to others."

How has anxiety influenced your academic or professional pursuits? Do you experience consistent concern regarding your work obligations? Have you withdrawn from your educational pursuits or resigned from employment due to a phobia of venturing outside? Have you refrained from enrolling in courses or pursuing occupations that require the practice of public speaking? Has the presence of work-related stress been a contributing factor to the development of your anxiety?

Consider the manner in which anxiety has influenced your academic or professional pursuits. What are your thoughts on your present academic or professional circumstances? Record your thoughts in the space below.

Health and Well-Being

Anne was experiencing both physical and psychological distress. She frequently experienced headaches that appeared to exacerbate in times of anxiousness. During her childhood, she derived pleasure from engaging in various sporting activities; however, in her adult years, she seldom participated in any form of physical exercise. A perpetual concern invariably arose that impeded her engagement in daily existence. Frequently, she experienced feelings of melancholy and a sense of stagnation, perceiving no prospects for change. It appeared that she was merely endeavoring to endure each passing day.

Anxiousness can exert an adverse influence on one's physical health and overall welfare. It has the potential to hinder your capacity to uphold your physical well-being, such as adhering to a balanced dietary regimen or engaging in consistent physical activity. Health conditions can exacerbate anxiety problems, including instances where asthma attacks lead to the manifestation of panic symptoms. Anxiety frequently co-occurs with migraines and irritable bowel syndrome, leading to potential distress and discomfort. It is possible that you may also experience concurrent mental health conditions, including but not limited to depression or substance use disorders, which can exacerbate the challenges associated with overcoming anxiety.

Let us take a moment to contemplate your overarching health and wellness. Have you received any medical diagnoses or been diagnosed with any mental health conditions that could potentially factor into the manifestation of your anxiety? How is your sleep? Do you consume a wholesome diet? Exercise regularly? Anxiety can exert a profound influence across these various realms of your life, and reciprocally, these spheres can equally affect your anxiety levels. Hence, it is imperative to assess your overall well-being. Write your thoughts below.

Daily Responsibilities

Anne encountered challenges in completing her daily responsibilities. Right from the start of her day, she exhibited a steadfast fixation on potential negative outcomes. She found it challenging to maintain focus on her domestic duties, resulting in excessive time spent on mundane tasks, such as the selection of her daily attire.

This classification encompasses activities that are typically conducted on a daily basis, such as operating a motor vehicle, preparing meals, engaging in personal hygiene, managing financial obligations, maintaining household cleanliness, deciding on attire, among others. Anxiety may impede one's capacity to perform fundamental tasks.

How proficient are you in meeting the requirements of everyday tasks? Does the presence of anxiety impede your ability to accomplish tasks? Do your jam-packed and intense daily schedules exacerbate your anxiety? Please document your thoughts in the designated area provided.

Methods For Releasing Inner Trust

There is a consistent concern regarding the occurrences in everyday circumstances. Nevertheless, the perpetual state of worry, constant anticipation of unfavorable outcomes, and perpetual indulgence in negative thoughts can have a debilitating effect and adversely impact both your physical and emotional well-being.

From an emotional standpoint, it has the potential to deplete your emotional resilience and induce feelings of restlessness, anxiety, lack of focus, and irritability. From a physical standpoint, individuals may experience symptoms such as headaches, increased abdominal stress, heightened muscle tension, and difficulties with sleep, including insomnia. Your level of focus and attention will be significantly challenged in both professional and educational environments.

One may exhibit hostility towards those in close proximity, experience pessimistic ideations, or resort to substance abuse, involving drugs, alcohol, or both, as a means of self-medication.

A substantial portion of individuals possess a personality trait commonly referred to as trust propensity. They begin by extending trust upon initial acquaintance. This arises from personal encounters and is rooted in a fundamental perspective concerning the reliability of individuals. The act of extending trust to individuals who are unfamiliar to us is inherent to our fundamental principles regarding the nature of existence. For individuals within the prevailing cultural framework, accomplishing this is comparatively uncomplicated, whereas for those who have experienced the breach of their trust, the task becomes significantly more challenging. The anticipation of trust should not be presumed without careful consideration.

Certain individuals tend to characterize trust as an attribute that necessitates being acquired through one's actions and behavior. This signifies an initial standpoint or perception characterized by absence or minimal trust, necessitating the establishment of trust from its very foundation. We regard trust as a bestowed gift onto individuals. They have the option to retain and cultivate this ability, or relinquish it. We commence from a foundation of faith, which has the potential to develop, broaden, or deteriorate. In the event of loss, retrieval becomes a challenge.

When engaging with individuals whom you encounter in non-professional or social settings, you have the opportunity to consciously choose your initial approach: harboring minimal or no trust, or embracing an amicable mindset that encompasses genuine trust. By being mindful, you would have the capacity to deliberately select which position you would prefer to adopt instead of automatically falling into one or the other.

Day 6

Exercise:

Clean something slowly. Please allocate ample time to complete the cleaning tasks, ensuring meticulous attention to detail and refraining from hurrying. You have the opportunity to tidy up various areas including your room, car, kitchen, bathroom, bag, desk drawer, and even your shoes—essentially, any space that requires cleaning. Proceed at a reduced pace while exerting complete focus on the task at hand. Discard as many items as feasible.

The majority of individuals hold a disdain for the act of cleaning and tend to engage in it solely when the disarray has reached an extreme level. Nevertheless, it is widely acknowledged that cleaning possesses tremendous therapeutic value, as we develop an emotional attachment to our disorderliness. Regular cleaning is a commendable endeavor as it entails the intentional elimination of disarray in the immediate context, thereby demonstrating a highly pragmatic approach.

Just as a disordered kitchen can give rise to a sense of chaos, the human mind can be subject to anxiety due to the presence of cluttered negative thoughts. It is important to bear in mind that anxiety stems from an inclination towards disordered thoughts centered around future events. Therefore, individuals who frequently experience anxiety tend to burden their minds and bodies with pressures that hinder genuine perception of the present moment. The sole manner in which one can eradicate this form of cognitive clutter is via the processes of observation, comprehension, and mindfulness.

The exercises contained within this book are intended to assist in alleviating the strain and confusion caused by anxiety, thus enabling one to attain a state of mental clarity. Should you not have already encountered it, the sensation of awakening to a life devoid of anxiety proves to be invigorating and captivating.

Engaging in a period of introspective calmness and concentrated respiration for a duration of 10 minutes. Recite the affirmation: "I am in a state of cleanliness." My thoughts are coherent."

(Please consider documenting and discussing this personal journey by utilizing the hashtag #30DaysClean)

Day 7

Exercise:

The majority of food items are equipped with a "Nutritional Information" label that provides details regarding the percentage of fat, cholesterol, sodium, carbohydrates, protein, and other significant components conducive to nutrition within the given product. Let us craft one tailored to your unique experience.

Please take a piece of paper and jot down the following terms: happiness, stress, anxiety, worry, anger, and depression. Please feel at liberty to include additional vocabulary that conveys the various emotions and sensations that you commonly encounter. Next, please indicate the corresponding percentages that most accurately represent the significance of these words in your personal experience. There is no inherent correctness or incorrectness in relation to this exercise; the objective is to gain a heightened level of consciousness concerning the prevailing emotions and feelings you frequently encounter. If one were to express a rating of 70% depression, it should not be regarded as inherently negative. One should strive to accurately acknowledge and accept these percentages by candidly representing them.

Which emotions garnered the most substantial proportions? Which received the lowest? Please bear in mind that your emotions and feelings do not define your identity. Nevertheless, it is important to acknowledge that you do undergo emotional experiences, and certain emotions may prevail more prominently than others. If you find yourself frequently encountering negative emotions rather than positive ones, do not let it perturb you. Regardless of the emotional state you may be encountering at present, diligently observe it and allow it to naturally dissipate. For the recurring negative emotions, assess them and allow them to diminish. Insight is integral to acquiring comprehension.

Ten minutes dedicated to tranquility and deliberate deep breathing. Recite the affirmation: "I am not governed by my emotions." I am present in the current moment."

I kindly invite you to share this experience by utilizing the hashtag #30DaysMyLabel.

Day 8

Exercise:

Select a musical composition and give it your undivided attention. You are welcome to select a song from your personal repertoire of music; alternatively, you may elect to activate the radio and anticipate the commencement of a musical composition.

When engaged in the act of song appreciation, refrain from focusing on the individual components of notes, beats, voice, or rhythm, but rather direct your attention towards the absence of sound that exists between each auditory element. Pay attention to the interruptions, breaks, and moments of silence between the musical notes. Attend to the absence of sound within the musical composition.

Have you ever come to the realization that the existence of your preferred musical compositions would be rendered impossible in the absence of periods of silence? Each musical element, whether it be a note, rhythm, beat, or voice, requires a brief pause to come into existence, even if that pause lasts for a fraction of a second. Absence of silence would result in the absence of noise, let alone the existence of music. This is not to imply that noise and silence are at odds; on the contrary, they complement each other. Sounds and silence form a harmonious relationship. Did you have the opportunity to perceive the absence of sound amidst the melody? Rehearse this action consistently every time you engage with music. Be attentive to the absence of sound that allows the music to persevere.

In a similar vein, it is imperative that we embrace silence to allow the inherent rhythm of existence to fully unveil itself.

Regrettably, numerous individuals are confronted with this challenge, as we reside in an imbalanced society that promotes noise rather than tranquility. Do not succumb to the influence of crowds driven by superficial trends, and do not be apprehensive of periods of silence. Quietude possesses potent healing qualities. Engage in the daily habit of maintaining silence; this will allow you to perceive and appreciate new and marvelous experiences. The feeling of anxiety dissipates within the realm of stillness.

An interval of 10 minutes dedicated to maintaining silence and engaging in concentrated breath control. Recite the mantra: "Maintain silence." Listen. Be silent."

(Please share your personal experience by using the hashtag #30DaysSilentSong)

Do you identify as an introvert or an extrovert?

In the 1920s, Carl Jung, during his examination of the various psychological orientations exhibited by individuals, introduced the terms 'extrovert' and 'introvert'. In his research, he emphasized that the disparities between the two can be attributed to a single determinant: energy. As per his assertion, extroverts derive their energy from social interactions, whereas such interactions can actually be draining for individuals who identify as introverts. This implies that individuals with introverted tendencies may require a period of solitude in order to replenish their energy levels following their participation in a social event, such as a party.

In essence, individuals categorized as extroverts are commonly perceived as sociable and gregarious in their interactions with the external environment. Introverts are characterized as individuals who exhibit a contemplative disposition, preferring solitude and directing their attention inward to engage with their mental or internal realm. Nevertheless, Jung himself acknowledged the absence of individuals who are entirely extroverted or introverted, as this notion does not align with reality.

However, there are individuals who display a greater inclination towards extroversion or introversion, or sometimes a combination of both, thereby categorizing them as "ambiverts" It was distinctly elucidated by Carl Jung that the existence of a purely extroverted or introverted individual is highly implausible. This implies that the majority of individuals can be categorized within the centroid of the continuum. Thus, it is common for individuals to exhibit a combination of extroverted and introverted inclinations.

Numerous researchers have elucidated that extroverts and introverts exhibit discernable dissimilarities in the functioning of their cerebral hemispheres. Extroverted individuals exhibit a propensity for embracing risk, pursuing new experiences, and deriving greater pleasure from unexpected or unfamiliar situations as compared to their counterparts. This can be correlated with their genetic composition, as well as the dopamine secretion within their brain. Additionally, the amygdala assumes responsibility for processing emotional stimuli within the brain. This phenomenon is evident in the exuberance or eagerness displayed by extroverts when engaging in highly stimulating activities, which may provoke a contrasting response in introverts such as overwhelming emotions resembling anxiety.

Additionally, there exists a discrepancy in the stimulus processing between introverted individuals and extroverted individuals. This suggests that the processing of brain stimulation varies depending on an individual's personality. For individuals who possess introverted tendencies, sensory input traverses a convoluted and protracted neural route within the cerebral regions associated with cognitive processes such as strategic thinking, recollection, and analytical reasoning. Contrarily, extroverts exhibit abridged brain pathways that traverse the regions of the brain linked to auditory, tactile, gustatory, visual, and sensory processing.

What is the degree of your extroversion or introversion?

An individual who possesses exclusively introverted or extroverted traits is exceedingly rare. In order to gain a comprehensive understanding of one's inclination towards either extroversion or introversion, it is essential to possess the knowledge required to distinguish between the two.

The Extroverts

Extroverts are regarded as individuals who have an affinity for socializing and engaging with others. They experience heightened vitality in the presence of others. An enjoyable evening for them would entail the presence of a dozen family members or close acquaintances. They possess a delightful sense of humor, exude warmth, and radiate energy, often assuming the role of the center of attention in social gatherings. They may, on occasion, exhibit self-centered and demanding traits, and will employ all means necessary to attain prominence.

Extroverted individuals effortlessly establish connections with unfamiliar individuals. They possess the ability to effortlessly engage in conversation with anyone when entering a social gathering. By the conclusion of the evening, it is likely that they will have interacted with no fewer than two or three individuals. Individuals with an extroverted temperament consistently seek stimulation due to their propensity to become easily bored. Tasks that involve repetition may prove tiresome to individuals, unless accompanied by a form of incentive, such as receiving acknowledgment or recognition. Furthermore, introverts exhibit longer attention spans in comparison to their extroverted counterparts.

Extroverts display great enthusiasm for their ideas, even if they have not been thoroughly deliberated upon. The process of generating and considering various ideas is usually an integral aspect of their cognitive deliberation. It appears that they exhibit a higher propensity for changing their viewpoints in contrast to an introverted individual.

Would you consider yourself to be categorized as an extrovert?

Examine these five prominent indicators of this particular personality profile:

1. You love talking

Extroverted individuals derive pleasure from engaging in conversation with their family members, friends, colleagues, neighbors, and even unfamiliar individuals. They have a strong affinity for acquiring knowledge about the lives of others and developing new friendships. Introverted individuals have a tendency to engage in extensive contemplation prior to verbalizing their thoughts, while extroverted individuals use spoken discourse as a means to structure and expand upon their ideas and thoughts. Additionally, extroverts possess an extensive social network due to their aptitude in connecting with individuals and initiating discussions.

2. Individuals with an extroverted nature exhibit a preference for engaging in discussions with the intention of generating viable solutions to problems.

Individuals characterized by extroversion typically exhibit a preference for engaging in discourse pertaining to the problem at hand, as well as exploring potential avenues for resolution through collaborative discussions with others. Engaging in a thorough discourse facilitates their identification of the underlying cause of the issue and enables them to determine the optimal course of action for its resolution. In contrast, introverts are inclined towards solitary contemplation when faced with a problem.

3. Social interaction invigorates extroverted individuals and serves as a source of motivation and creativity.

After socializing, extroverts experience a heightened sense of motivation and energy. Social interactions can impart a significant sense of rejuvenation to individuals of their inclination. Extended periods of solitary confinement can lead to feelings of ennui and a lack of creative motivation. They consistently exhibit a preference for socializing with a collective or assembly of individuals.

4. They are receptive to interacting with others.

Extroverted individuals possess a strong inclination towards openness and exhibit a consistent willingness to express their emotions and ideas. They are readily discernible in contrast to introverts, who tend to be distant and frequently reserved.

5. They exhibit an amiable demeanor and are easily accessible.

Individuals with extroverted tendencies frequently engage in social interaction, thereby exhibiting a heightened level of approachability. They will assume the initiative to commence introductions and engage in conversations at the event. This facilitates their ability to establish new social connections.

Positivity Challenge

The objective of the positivity challenge is to encourage individuals to engage in positive thinking with greater frequency compared to their previous mindset. This clearly represents the utmost imperative in the development of emotional intelligence—by embarking on this endeavor, you are effectively enhancing your ability to predominantly cultivate positive thinking patterns. This notion aims to inspire individuals to adopt a more regular practice of positive thinking, cultivating a habitual pattern of engaging in positive thoughts. By participating in this challenge, you are essentially compelling yourself to adopt a mindset of positive thinking.

The difficulty lies in the fact that whenever a pessimistic thought arises, it becomes crucial to counter it with two additional optimistic thoughts. It is imperative that the positive thoughts be connected to the subject matter that was previously causing negative thoughts, thus compelling oneself to seek the positive aspects even in unfavorable circumstances or those that were strongly disliked. By acknowledging the affirmative aspects, you instill in your mind the habit of positive thinking.

For instance, consider the scenario in which you decided to patronize a recently established pizzeria in close proximity to your residence. It was extensively promoted, leading you to consider giving it a try. Upon consumption, you unraveled that the prominent ploy lay in its composition, involving a cauliflower crust, a revelation that led to your aversion towards it. I discovered myself evaluating the subpar quality of the food and harboring a vehement dislike towards it. By entertaining that pessimistic thought, you subsequently found it necessary to actively embrace two optimistic thoughts pertaining to the pizza. One potential reason could be your expression of gratitude for the opportunity to consume a wholesome and nourishing meal, acknowledging the inherent nutritional benefits of consuming a dish primarily composed of vegetables. The subsequent consideration would thus be the attainment of regular sustenance in the initial instance. You acknowledge the existence of multiple individuals who suffer from food insecurity and lack the same level of accessibility to food as you do. Upon actively embracing these positive thoughts, you come to the realization that the situation was not entirely negative, and that dining at that establishment had the potential to be considerably worse.

Comprehending Nonverbal Communication

When it comes to enhancing one's ability to interpret the nonverbal cues displayed by individuals, there are two key actions to consider. Firstly, one endeavors to learn the art of deciphering others' body language, enabling them to gain insights into their thoughts and emotions during any specific instance. In addition, it is imperative to ensure that you cultivate the necessary competencies to effectively align your behavior with the specific emotional state you desire to embody. It is imperative to adopt a mindset of "acting as if" until one achieves the desired outcome. By actively acquiring the skill of interpreting others' body language, one gains the capacity to effectively employ body language techniques aligned with particular mindsets. Additionally, you can expand upon this concept by cultivating the ability to discern your own nonverbal cues, comprehending their underlying significance. Through this practice, you gain a deeper insight into your own emotional states, particularly during moments of difficulty in interpreting them accurately.

Utilization of Methodologies

ACT techniques frequently employ metaphors, paradoxes, and experiential exercises. There exist numerous strategies that exhibit qualities of playfulness, imagination, and intelligence. ACT procedures can vary in duration, encompassing both brief interventions lasting a few minutes to more extensive treatments spanning multiple sessions. In accordance with the designated set of five principles, a range of methodologies can be classified based on the clinical materials accumulated by Gifford, Hayes, and Stroshal (2005).

1. Examining the prevailing circumstances or the phenomenon known as "creative hopelessness" enables clients to gain insight into their endeavors, assess the true extent of their achievements, and establish an opportunity for alternative outcomes. When faced with the impracticability of

their numerous encounters, individuals often find themselves in a state of "creative hopelessness," uncertain about the subsequent course of action. The circumstance is characterized by ingenuity as it allows for the generation of entirely novel methodologies, independent of any preexisting regulations dictating their operations.

2. Acceptance strategies have been devised with the intent of mitigating or minimizing drive in order to circumvent the emergence of said conditions. The concept of "disengagement" is underscored - acknowledging the fact that thoughts and emotions do not invariably influence behaviors. Group interactions are commonly structured through the use of in vivo techniques. Significant importance is placed on distinguishing between emotions, sentiments, and encounters.

3. The process of cognitive deliteralization in defusion serves to redefine thought and experience as an ongoing behavioral process, rather than merely a final outcome. Strategies are formulated to demonstrate that concepts are subjective perceptions or mental intuitions, devoid of concrete substantiation. One possibility could be: "It may require sitting closely alongside the client and offering a comprehensive representation of all ideas and viewpoints as a unified entity in an effort to mitigate tensions and mitigate literal interpretations."

4. Placing emphasis on preferences provides a clear understanding of the individual's intrinsic needs, specifically, what bestows significance upon their existence? The objective is to assist clients in deciphering the differentiation between a value and an objective, choosing their values and communicating them, and establishing

behavioral goals that align with said values.

5. The concept of self, when considered within its contextual framework, enables individuals to perceive their own identity as separate from the substance of their encounters.

Effective ACT Interventions for Optimal Outcomes

Creative Hopelessness

Incorporating innovative approaches to addressing clients' challenges, creative hopelessness strategies enable individuals to discern areas of improvement and develop actionable plans aimed at accomplishing their objectives. These methodologies, commonly referred to as 'strategies for addressing the current circumstances,' encompass elements of understanding, self-reflection, and thoughtful analysis. The aforementioned abilities are designated as creative, as they foster the exploration of novel and untried pursuits.

Creative hopelessness imparts to the individual the understanding that, ultimately, they must confront and address the prevailing circumstances. This methodology promotes the individual's willingness to acknowledge the truth, extending well beyond the cultivation of evasive tendencies. He must acknowledge the state of hopelessness and subsequently forge a fresh trajectory. He must construct a more buoyant and novel endeavor, one imbued with optimism. This tool has the capacity to assist individuals in attaining a more intimate understanding of their own intrinsic worth. It contributes to the preservation of tranquility and well-being among individuals, enabling the creation of fresh prospects within a favorable environment ideal for their realization.

Exploring the concept of Creative Despondency through the use of an Illustration

Let us examine a brief narrative to grasp the concept of creative hopelessness. It's a farmer\\\'s story. An individual presents him with an extraordinary employment opportunity that will bestow upon him significant benefits. The task entails exclusive engagement with a donkey and a shovel within the confines of a field. However, there is a minor condition: he must conceal his eyes.

The morally upright individual acknowledges the instructions given and abides by them. Nevertheless, he is unaware of the presence of gaps throughout the entire vicinity. The farmer has inadvertently fallen into one of the predetermined locations. The farmer removes his blindfold and, equipped with only his shovel, proceeds with uncertainty and without any knowledge of how to free himself. He engages in continuous excavation and tunnel construction for nearly an entire day. In due time, he realizes that his actions have merely exacerbated his predicament, propelling himself further into the abyss.

He assesses his situation upon realizing this and chooses an alternative course of action. He subsequently intends to employ the shovel in a distinct manner. This concise illustration exemplifies the essence of creative despair. Our personal tendencies to evade challenges serve to exacerbate our feelings of depression and further complicate the issues we face.

"What Makes Creative Hopelessness Such A Potent Tool?

The primary objective is for individuals to acknowledge the adverse encounters that they are incapable of effectively handling internally. They are expected to refrain from engaging in conflict with them, endeavor to elude their presence, and refrain from fixating on them excessively. Instead, individuals should embrace a sense of hopelessness and acknowledge the lack of meaning in their previous course of action while expressing their acceptance and willingness to move on by proclaiming, "I acknowledge and release it."

The counselor has the ability to offer guidance to the individual after acknowledging specific unpleasant or concerning information. This should be accomplished through a process of dialogue that fosters the exploration of alternative options or pathways, in conjunction with constructive motivation, a clear objective, and genuine optimism.

The therapist utilizes their empathetic skills to facilitate the individual's recognition of past adversities and their dispensability in the present moment. The sense of despair, nonetheless, can serve as a driving force. It can serve as a means to discover alternative solutions. It can be likened to an individual stepping back two paces in order to ascend to even greater heights.

Interventions for Enhancing Acceptance Skills

The cultivation of acceptance skills can be facilitated through various means such as engaging in discussions, employing role models, utilizing scenario-based activities, or employing distinct worksheets and exercises. The primary aim of acceptance strategies is to disengage individuals and convey to them that, especially when burdened by anguish and tension, not all thoughts must manifest as actions.

Acceptance strategies enable individuals to discern between beneficial and counterproductive sentiments, emotions, and behavioral tendencies.

Deliteralization Strategy

The phenomenon of deliteralization is intricately linked to the concept of cognitive defusion, contributing significantly to the reconfiguration of our cognitive and affective frameworks. Cognitive defusion techniques illustrate the ability to modify our perception of negativity, allowing us to overcome it without compromising its actual existence.

Operating autonomously from verbal communication.

Derived from the experiential practice developed by Monestès and Villatte (2013), this approach assists the client in exercising autonomy in spite of their thoughts. In a certain context, it can be viewed as a form of exposure that fosters the capacity to behave in accordance with one's convictions instead of spontaneously reacting to one's cognitive processes. Therefore, the objective pertains to acquiring psychological adaptability.

Values Intervention

Guiding clients on an emotional journey through their own funeral is a value-oriented endeavor designed to assist them in comprehending their personal beliefs and values. As a therapist, it would be advisable to prompt the client to envision a scenario where they have experienced an unforeseen demise, in order to initiate the dialogue. They shall partake in their own funeral proceedings, as dictated by societal conventions, albeit as a mere semblance of their former being.

This discourse presents an opportunity to delve into the elements that individuals desire to incorporate within the eulogies dedicated to their acquaintances, alongside the speeches delivered by their kin. What epitaph should be inscribed upon their gravestone? It may incite an examination into queries such as the ones below:

What is their intended outcome?

What kind of individual do they desire to be remembered as by others?
Which attributes will be discussed?
How might their contributions have positively impacted the lives of others or exerted significant influence on them?

15. Develop the skill of delaying or deferring the act of worrying.

We are all well aware of the challenges posed by the pervasive influence of worry and anxiety on our ability to maintain a high level of productivity. Is there any action we can take to rectify this situation? To commence, when anxious thoughts arise, they perpetually exhibit a sense of being beyond one's command. They effectively render you immobile, causing all your attempts to be futile. As an illustration, you can attempt employing logical arguments to alleviate concerns, diverting your attention to alternative activities, reciting constructive affirmations, cultivating optimistic thoughts, reviewing your list of things you are grateful for, and exploring a plethora of other techniques designed to foster a sense of tranquility. Regrettably, these thoughts may persist. This, in and of itself, may give rise to concern. One begins to experience distress and a heightened sense of unease regarding their elevated anxiety levels, often accompanied by feelings of powerlessness towards their circumstances. May I inquire as to what strategies you can employ in order to effectively address the problem at hand? The key lies in acquiring the skill to defer one's concerns. However, may I inquire about the means by which you plan to accomplish this task? Presented herein is a comprehensive, sequential elucidation on the methodology required to achieve this desired outcome.

Allot a designated interval for concerns: Rather than permitting worries to arise intermittently and persistently, you may establish a specific time and location reserved solely for the purpose of addressing them. As an example, you may allocate the time frame from 5pm to 5.20pm as a dedicated period in which you are entitled to express any concerns or anxieties you may have. Be sure to designate a particular zone of concern. As an example, it is acceptable to experience concern or unease in areas such as restrooms or any other location, but it is important to refrain from utilizing the bedroom for such purposes. Furthermore, it is important to avoid scheduling the allocated worry time too close to your bedtime to mitigate the risk of experiencing difficulties falling asleep. When the occasion to engage in contemplation presents itself, proceed to the designated place of reflection and carefully ponder any concerns recorded within your dedicated journal of anxieties. The remaining part of the day ought to be a period exempt from anxiety. What measures do you typically employ when intrusive thoughts arise? That is where the subsequent phase comes into play.

Postpone your worry. In the event that any distressing or concerning thoughts arise within your mind, please take care to record said worrisome thoughts on a piece of paper, and subsequently defer the act of worrying until a designated period of time specifically intended for addressing worries. Maintain a constant awareness that you shall be afforded ample opportunity to contemplate any troubling thoughts at their designated moment, thus absolving you of present concern. The advantage lies in the fact that you will be documenting them, alleviating any concerns about potential forgetfulness. Please make a written record of it and proceed with your day in the usual manner. When the need for concern arises, the subsequent course of action becomes relevant.

Carefully review the list of concerns that you have documented throughout the day, and allocate some dedicated time for deeply contemplating these worries. It is important to carefully contemplate the concerns that you have recorded throughout the day. After reviewing this list, you may proceed to engage in unrestricted worrying until the predetermined duration has elapsed. Consequently, it is imperative that you configure the alarm to prevent inadvertently being ensnared within the confines of your designated period for anxiety. However, if the concerns no longer hold significant importance, it is prudent to restrict the duration of your period of worry to a reasonable amount of time that you deem sufficient to address all matters.

What is the mechanism behind and rationale for this phenomenon? By deferring concern, one can enhance their ability to fully immerse themselves in the present moment, rather than expending energy on apprehending an uncertain future and lamenting a bygone past. Furthermore, the act of merely deferring your concerns implies that you need not expend excessive exertion to cease your current state of worry. You are aware that you have your designated time for concern, during which you may direct your focus towards any matter you deem necessary. The further you cultivate the practice of deferring your anxious thoughts, the more apparent it will become to you that you possess a significant level of influence over your worrying that you may not fully acknowledge.

Gaining Insight Into The Kinetics Of Human Physiology

Regarding the examination of the arms, a broader range of movements may occur compared to the analysis of the shoulders. This can be attributed to heightened levels of dexterity. In a broader sense, it can be observed that increased dexterity in a bodily appendage corresponds to enhanced capability for executing a greater variety of movements.

Crossing arms

The act of folding one's arms initiates an instant delineation that separates oneself from the individual situated in front. This unequivocally indicates your utter lack of interest in engaging with those in your vicinity. Upon examining the behavior of crossing one's arms, it becomes apparent that the individual intends to establish a certain degree of separation or protective barrier between themselves and the other person. Regard this individual as reserved and endeavor to gradually foster their openness.

Expanding arms outward

When one extends their arms outwards, they are engaging in one of several actions. It is possible that you are displaying a sense of contentment with the present circumstances. You seek to exhibit a sense of comfort to individuals around you, demonstrating a willingness to be receptive and open. Alternatively, it is plausible that your conduct demonstrates a taste for control or possibly even hostility, contingent upon the accompanying activities. Taking all factors into account, nevertheless, it is an authentic manifestation of unguarded nonverbal communication that ought to be understood in that manner.

Hiding arms

When you conceal your arms, you attempt to mask or obscure them in some manner. There are two possible actions that could be taken: either withdrawing them or readjusting them to provide support behind your back. Withdrawing can demonstrate defensiveness, while retaining a poised posture with hands casually positioned at the back can convey a sense of nonchalance and self-assurance. Regardless, it is essential to consider the fact that you are demonstrating such a high level of confidence.

Pulling arms inward

When you retract your arms, you are actively withdrawing from an interpersonal exchange. You are disengaging yourself, endeavoring to distance yourself from it. This behavior represents a clear manifestation of closed body language, indicative of a reluctance to continue engaging in the interaction. This matter ought to be treated with utmost seriousness.

Elevating the arms overhead

By extending your arms vertically, you enhance your apparent size. You may be engaging in excessive motion, or alternatively, displaying assertive behavior. Examine the remaining aspects of your body language and subsequently ensure their integration. Typically, one may infer that this phenomenon enhances or emphasizes corresponding indications conveyed by the remaining aspects of the individual's nonverbal communication as well.

Reaching out

When extending your arm towards another individual, the interpretation thereof depends fully on the underlying intention behind the action, as well as the degree of applied pressure. As a general rule, when an individual displays a vigorous approach in reaching out to someone, it often indicates an intention to cause harm. Conversely, when someone adopts a gentle and cautious manner while extending their hand, it typically signifies a deliberate effort to convey comfort or kindness. Please take note of the method of contact.

Self-hugging

Self-embracing is commonly employed as a means of self-comfort or consolation. Consider the appearance - you are extending your arm and clasping your side. You are demonstrating a demeanor of guardedness and making an effort to compose yourself. You are endeavoring to discover strategies to enhance your ability to unwind, thereby facilitating your increased participation. Alternatively, you are striving to maintain composure until you can extricate yourself from a situation that may not align with your desired standards.

Employing limbs as implements of combat.

By employing one's arms as implements of combat, one unequivocally indicates an unwillingness to engage with one's immediate surroundings. You are clearly expressing your desire for personal space. You are exhibiting confrontational behavior towards others. It may be deemed as an act of self-preservation, or alternatively, you might be regarded as the initiator. This is wholly contingent upon the particular circumstances. Nonetheless, it exhibits indications of aggression. The upper limbs possess the potential to function as an implement for striking when the hand is clenched. It can slap. It is capable of delivering punches or jabs. The hands possess immense potential as formidable tools for exerting force upon individuals.

Reading Hands

Ultimately, upon careful observation of individuals who prefer practical engagement, their motions and behavior reveal a wealth of untapped capabilities. Individuals commonly attempt to conceal their hands; nevertheless, hands possess a high degree of transparency, and this knowledge is widespread among the majority. Nevertheless, by cultivating attentiveness, one can discern the indicators that may signify a predicament requiring resolution.

Waving one's hands in the air

When executing the chopping maneuver, it is crucial to maintain a rigid, flat position of the hand as it is propelled swiftly and smoothly through the air. On occasion, you may intentionally strike the side of your hand against the center of your opposite palm. It is intended to convey a sense of supremacy. This holds particularly true if you perform the action while keeping your palms facing downwards. Nevertheless, adopting a hand gesture with your palms facing upward while chopping could potentially convey an intention to persuade others of your credibility.

Clasping hands together

When individuals interlock their hands, they are grasping their own hands. This behavior is commonly seen as a sign of self-restraint or an effort to achieve a state of composure. It is expected to demonstrate your intention to remain consistent. Typically, this conduct is commonly perceived as withdrawn, particularly when the hands remain rigid while in that position.

Hands hidden

The act of concealing one's hands suggests an intention to withhold information or obscure the truth. You are making an effort to conceal your hands, potentially by placing them behind your back or inside your pockets, in order to prevent others from reading them. This situation is characterized by a high level of guardedness and suggests the possibility of covert intentions. Alternatively, it may also indicate an intense inclination towards obedience and compliance.

Fingers clenched into closed fists

When exhibiting a clenched fist positioned at your sides, you demonstrate a resolute demeanor. It might be considered as confrontational if you exhibit additional instances of forceful conduct. In order to ascertain whether it is mere obstinacy or has the potential to escalate into overt aggression, it is imperative to provide adequate context.

Hands on hips

Assuming an open posture typically involves placing one's hands on the hips. While often misconstrued as hostility or assertiveness, it is in fact an attitude of preparedness for forthcoming events. It indicates your willingness to undertake any necessary tasks in the days to come.

The measurement of the thumb's vertical dimension.

Upon observation of the thumbs, it becomes apparent that confidence typically manifests in the form of elevated thumb placement. Consider the manner in which you may hold your arms when they are crossed. When your thumb is extended and directed outward, it indicates an aggressive upward direction.

Holding onto something

By retaining something, one typically establishes a form of protection or obstacle for oneself. Consider the visual impact of placing a mobile device or a beverage container as a physical barrier between oneself and another individual. One could maintain physical contact with the object, positioning it as a barrier to create a clear delineation between oneself and the other party.

Pointing

The act of gesturing with one's finger to indicate a specific direction or target is generally viewed as impolite. However, it is noteworthy that this behavior may also be suggestive of a display of authority or assertiveness in certain contexts. It signifies a manifestation of your superior command over a given circumstance or denotes your assertion of dominance over another individual.

Consider the manner in which you might reprimand a young child through the application of a raised index finger. It is intended to convey a sense of severity and reprimand.

Displaying one's hands openly with palms facing downwards

By extending your hands with the palms facing downwards, you are signaling an overt display of control over the situation. You are unequivocally asserting your authority over the current situation and adamantly declining any alterations to your course of action. You demonstrate unwavering resolve in the given circumstances, while simultaneously exhibiting a sincere commitment to transparency. This occurrence is frequently observed when analyzing the interaction between politicians or leaders and a multitude of individuals.

Exhibiting hands in a visible manner with palms facing upwards.

When one displays their hands openly, with the palms facing upwards, it is indicative of one's sincerity and integrity. Specifically, this is an appeal for confidence, demonstrating your complete transparency and absence of any ulterior motives within the given circumstances. You are demonstrating a desire to be regarded as being truthful presently. This phenomenon is frequently observed among pastors or priests while delivering a sermon.

Steepling fingers

When you interlace your fingers, the pads of your fingers are firmly pressed together, but the palms and lengths of the fingers never make contact. It bears a striking resemblance to the appearance of a rooftop spire positioned above an individual. It is intended to demonstrate a portrayal of assurance and supremacy. This is a conspicuous indication of superiority. It is typically observed by individuals in positions of authority convened around a conference table, employing a deliberate and analytical approach.

The thermal condition of the hands.

The thermal characteristics exhibited by your hands can provide valuable insight into the current sensory experience. Typically, heightened body tension can be observed when there is a decrease in hand temperature. This occurs due to the physiological response of the body to stress, wherein blood flow is directed towards critical regions such as the cardiovascular system, while the lower extremities are engorged to facilitate swift movement. Nevertheless, in cases where the hands are warmer, it generally indicates indications of easing tension. This gains further significance when considering the field of haptics.

Widened hands

The display of comfort is indicated when the hands are held in a spacious position. This indicates that if the observer can discern distinct intervals between each finger or if the hands are noticeably distanced from one another. This can be typically observed by discerning the significant breadth between the fingers upon stretching them out. A narrower hand width is indicative of heightened levels of stress.

Does Cognitive Behavioral Therapy Have Advantages and Disadvantages?

Although it demonstrates comparable efficacy to the methods employed in treating officially recognized mental illnesses, it is important to acknowledge that individual responses may vary, as what may be beneficial for one person might not be suitable for another individual with psychologically-induced behavioral patterns.

The advantages include:

The duration of treatment can be comparatively briefer in comparison to alternative therapeutic approaches.

It may serve as the sole recourse in cases where medical treatments prove ineffective.

There exist a multitude of approaches to its presentation, encompassing the engagement of a therapist, utilization of self-help literature, or reliance on applications.

The skills imparted have practical utility in the context of everyday life, and this remains applicable even subsequent to therapy.

The disadvantages include:
Increased collaboration and dedication are imperative, given the protracted nature of the undertaking.

Significant time expenditure, particularly when professional intervention and additional tasks are involved.

A conflict between emotions and thoughts is present in this situation, thus causing one to inevitably encounter a certain degree of uneasiness at the onset.

Complicated mental conditions may require additional support and intervention. At this juncture, cognitive behavioral therapy may not be efficacious.

Here are the Key Points to Remember

Cognitive Behavioral Therapy (CBT) is rooted in scientific evidence, thereby substantiating its efficacy.

Cognitive Behavioral Therapy introduces novel cognitive and behavioral strategies to enhance our mindset and actions. This text offers a valuable resource for self-improvement and guidance in addressing such concerns.

Our thoughts, emotions, and actions are intrinsically linked, forming an intricate cycle of interconnection. Altering one element results in influencing the remainder.

The Significance Of Adverse Thinking

As previously stated, cognitive behavioral therapy operates on the principle that our emotions are not solely determined by external circumstances, but rather by the subjective interpretations we assign to those circumstances. Consequently, if one's cognitive patterns tend toward negativity, it can impede the process of making lucid and dependable choices.

An exemplary case would be that of a student who has obtained subpar grades on an examination. It is undeniable that this will inevitably lead the student to experience feelings of depression and stress. Nevertheless, the student's ultimate choice will be influenced by their perception of said occurrence. Having a positive mindset will enable the student to perceive failure as an opportunity for growth, inspiring them to exert greater effort in order to attain higher levels of accomplishment.

Conversely, pessimistic thoughts can significantly alter a student's perception of themselves, their surroundings, and possibly even the entire world. The student may develop a belief that he or she lacks capability and potential in various aspects of life, which can subsequently lead to contemplating extreme, irreversible actions, such as suicide.

Notwithstanding, peculiar as it may seem, negative thoughts generally possess a degree of significance. Upon careful examination, it can be observed that individuals with a pessimistic mindset often fail to confront life's realities as they truly are. Alternatively, they endeavor to evade the realities of existence.

Let us consider the aforementioned example. The student may have chosen to adopt a mindset of optimism and contemplated the worst-case scenario, subsequently proceeding as if it were the most profound counsel they had received. Nevertheless, this would not be advantageous as such optimistic thoughts have a tendency to imply that we have already accomplished our goals, thereby promoting complacency. Consequently, this viewpoint prevents us from attaining or realizing our complete capabilities in life.

From Whence Do These Pessimistic Thoughts Originate?

It is commonly held that negative thoughts tend to stem from beliefs acquired during one's formative years. As we progress, these beliefs become ingrained within us, forming deep-rooted and automatic patterns of thought. How is this possible?

For instance, let us consider a child whose upbringing instills the belief that success in life necessitates achieving satisfactory grades in academic examinations. This is a commonly used phrase that is familiar to all individuals.

However, this notion gives rise to heightened psychological strain in children, as their failures may give birth to detrimental self-doubt, such as questioning their inherent abilities or prospects of future success. These are examples of the negative cognitions under discussion. Frequently, these thoughts arise organically and spontaneously as a result of the held convictions.

In such instances, adopting a different set of convictions tends to be the most effective course of action to rectify such thought patterns. Cognitive therapy typically becomes applicable in this context. Cognitive behavioral therapy facilitates the development of alternative perspectives in these situations. Regarding the aforementioned child, he or she will have the capacity to venture forth and investigate alternative courses of action to pursue in the event of an unsuccessful test outcome.

It is crucial to comprehend that adverse events are inevitable in this section. However, the key inquiry to pose is how one intends to approach the confrontation.

Reveal The Underlying Factors That Elicit Stress

In the event that you were to visit the emergency room expressing discomfort due to abdominal cramps, the medical professionals would not solely administer pain medication and discharge you. They would diligently conduct an inquiry into your symptoms, in order to devise an appropriate course of action to facilitate your recovery. The treatment of stress and anxiety is identical.

In order to effectively address the overwhelming sensation, it is imperative to identify the underlying cause. This aims to achieve this objective by offering you a substantive assessment in the form of a practical quiz, aiding you in the identification of stimuli that trigger your negative thoughts. Let's get started.

Triggers Versus Causes

Triggers are distinct entities compared to causes – envision them akin to a theatrical production on Broadway. The causes are the elements that establish the groundwork for the performance - they serve as the director, issuing instructions to the actors, guiding their emotional portrayal, setting the backdrop, and frequently commanding attention if afforded the opportunity.

But triggers are different. The aforementioned actions are the ones perceptible on the stage. They represent the captivating narrative that unfolds in front of your eyes. These are the occurrences that the characters undergo, the interpersonal connections that are brutally torn apart; they encompass all of the plot developments. They frequently serve as the decisive factor that culminates in negative consequences.

Now, let us redirect our focus towards you to gain deeper insights into your inner workings and identify the factors that may cause vulnerability, through the exploration of the forthcoming questionnaire.

Quiz: Identifying Factors that Elicit Stress and Anxiety

Please respond to the following inquiries with sincerity, dedicating adequate thought to each answer. There exists no definitive correct or incorrect responses; rather, the opportunity arises to attain a deeper comprehension of oneself. Assign a numerical rating on a scale of 1 to 5 for each question, where 1 represents the lowest rating and 5 represents the highest rating.

Thus, allocate a few moments to settle yourself with a preferred warm beverage and commence your endeavors.

1) Do you frequently experience a sense of being overwhelmed by the demands of life?

2) Have you ever encountered challenges when attempting to arise from your slumber in the morning?

3) What level of satisfaction do you experience in regard to your life?

4) On a scale from 1 to 10, what level would you assign to your self-esteem?

5) Are you accustomed to prioritizing the needs of others over your own?

6) Are you experiencing feelings of irritability and stress in relation to individuals in your vicinity?

Are you accustomed to taking a lunch break?

Could you please indicate whether or not you vacate your desk during your lunch break?

9) Do you frequently encounter challenges when it comes to adhering to project timelines?

10) Do you engage in regular disputes with your significant other?

11) Does the behavior of your children or family members incite you to exhibit anger or frustration?

Could you please confirm if you serve as a caregiver?

13) Do you hold yourself to a high degree of excellence?

14) Does the matter of finances pose a concern for you?

15) Are you frequently inclined to desire a greater allocation of hours within the span of a day?

Could you please share your level of satisfaction with your current occupation?

17) Do you feel content with your physical appearance?

Could you please confirm if your desk is organized?

19) Are you bothered by untidiness?

Could you please identify the three primary factors that contribute to your experience of stress?

....

....

....

21) Are you anticipating the upcoming holiday season?

Considering the nature of human fallibility, how do you manage the process of rectifying an error on your part?

23) Are there any particular concerns that cause you apprehension?

Please be aware that there is no definitive or erroneous response to this question, but instead, it should be approached with a spirit of inquiry and comprehension.

Maintaining a stress or anxiety journal for a duration of approximately two weeks can also be highly beneficial. Whenever you experience stress or anxiety, it is advisable to document the respective event in this journal, alongside the accompanying symptoms and the trigger that caused it. This effectively aids in enhancing your recollection of the intricate particulars, fostering an ability to adopt a detached and impartial stance towards your experience.

Positive Emotions

Negative emotions often receive a significant amount of focus, giving the impression that positive emotions are scarce. Nevertheless, this perception does not reflect reality. Additionally, the field of psychology has devoted considerable effort to exploring solutions for issues stemming from negative emotions, rather than focusing on the positive aspects of individuals' lives.

Positive emotions are characterized as sentiments devoid of negativity, such as the absence of any unpleasant or distressing aspects associated with an emotion. Research has consistently demonstrated that individuals must maintain a proportion of three instances of positive emotions for every one instance of negative emotions in order to attain overall well-being. The prevalent affirmative sentiments that have been recognized encompass gratitude, pride, hope, amusement, joy, interest, awe, serenity, love, and inspiration. There exist several additional positive emotions that merit consideration, such as the sentiment an individual experiences when providing assistance to others, contentment, or a sense of alleviation.

The correlation between gratitude and happiness is profound as individuals who possess gratitude simply direct their attention towards the positives in their life, rather than excessively dwelling on their wants and desires.

As an individual's sense of gratitude grows more profound, it serves not only to reinforce their positive mindset but also to nurture their altruistic inclination to aid others. A constructive outlook can further prompt an individual to contemplate upon their sincere appreciation and contemplate on leveraging their present contentment to achieve amplified happiness in the days to come.

Pride can encompass both positive and negative aspects within the realm of human emotions. An individual who is deemed prideful is likewise perceived as being arrogant or prioritizing their own interests above those of others. This implies that while an individual characterized by excessive pride may experience personal satisfaction, it is likely to come at the detriment of others.

The affirmative aspect of pride is marked by the sense of satisfaction and gratification that an individual derives from their own accomplishments or the achievements of their team. The affirmative facet of pride is regarded as the more pristine manifestation of this sentiment, as it arises organically without any disparagement towards others.

Hope can be regarded as a proactive manifestation of happiness. Put simply, it refers to the gratification an individual experiences when contemplating the potential occurrence of favorable circumstances in their forthcoming life.

Hope serves as a doorway through which individuals can embark upon a journey towards the attainment of happiness and other uplifting sentiments in their forthcoming endeavors.

The positive sentiment of hope is intricately linked to optimism and one's inherent inclination to perceive favorable aspects in situations. This tendency enables individuals to transform unhappy circumstances by channeling their efforts towards contemplating how they can enhance the situation.

Amusement is the emotional response that arises when an individual encounters humor. One potential alternative in a formal tone could be: "They could be subjected to a humorous anecdote or witness an unforeseen event within the natural environment, instigating a perception of amusement in their surroundings."

Entertainment, in fact, represents one of the most accessible methods for individuals to establish connections with others, as engaging in shared laughter can substantiate interpersonal ties. Amusement is also advantageous for individuals endeavoring to cultivate a lighthearted perspective, particularly with regard to oneself. If an individual possesses the capacity to derive amusement from their own errors, they are capable of acquiring the ability to attain contentment even in the aftermath of their most profound hardships.

Furthermore, the elevated sentiment of joy encompasses a spectrum of emotions, spanning from a state of contentment to an overwhelming sense of euphoria. Joy is arguably among the most frequently recognized positive emotions, owing perhaps to its status as one of the most coveted emotional states as well. Nevertheless, elation is typically a transitory sensation, occurring expeditiously yet dissipating just as swiftly.

Joy can be derived from a multitude of positive emotional states as positive emotions are inherently connected to feelings of happiness. Nevertheless, it is advantageous to distinguish and discern the various positive emotions in order to gain a genuine understanding of one's current emotional state. There is a prevailing belief that the level of happiness experienced by an individual can be heightened once they have successfully discovered aspects of life that bring them immense joy.

Interest encompasses the constructive sentiment that individuals leverage to fulfill their essential requisites and aspirations throughout their existence. This sentiment is further shaped by an individual's inclination to explore novelty within their surroundings. From a certain perspective, one could argue that interest can be regarded as a manifestation of arousal. When an individual demonstrates a genuine curiosity towards their surroundings, they concurrently engage in the exploration of unexplored delights that life has to offer.

Awe is the emotion experienced by an individual upon witnessing the sun descending over the water or upon entering a completely renovated apartment that resonates with their personal taste and adoration. It encapsulates the emotions experienced by an individual upon hearing their preferred musician passionately perform their most beloved composition. The sentiment of astonishment can be encountered and esteemed through artistic portrayals, artistic manifestations, and various mediums of imaginative articulation.

The sensation of profound wonderment is likewise experienced on a spiritual level. Take, for instance, the scenario where one is captivated by the magnificence of their deity or the boundless expanse of the cosmos. When an individual experiences a sense of awe, they are cultivating a receptive mindset and physical state to embrace novel experiences, resulting in enhanced happiness. Their attention is directed towards their external surroundings, internal sensations, and anything perceptible, thereby fostering this profound emotional state.

Serenity is the emotional state that arises when an individual is fully satisfied with their present circumstances. Serenity is essentially the state that ensues when an individual experiences an absence of both physical and mental anguish. This can be partially attributed to the correlation between serenity and the individual's spiritual state characterized by a sense of unity with the cosmos, as opposed to perceiving oneself as a mere subject or recipient of destiny.

Love is a prominent affirmative sentiment frequently recognized due to its influential nature, as it unfolds during infancy towards either one's parents or caregivers.

Nevertheless, love is a profoundly intricate sentiment that manifests itself in various manifestations, occasionally met with reciprocity, while at other instances remaining unrequited. It is widely acknowledged that the highest manifestation of love is characterized by its unconditionality, whereby individuals strive to give selflessly without any expectation of reciprocation. The love that is shared between individuals in a romantic context entails a reciprocal exchange of affection.

The ultimate and most discernible positive emotion can be identified as inspiration. This specific sentiment arises within an individual upon witnessing another person achieve a goal or listening to an exceptionally compelling speech, subsequently instilling within the observer a sense of inspiration to pursue a distinct path in their own life.

Hence, inspiration possesses significant persuasive power, rendering it highly valuable in the task of altering individuals' perspectives. With that being acknowledged, it is widely recognized that leaders are inclined to employ their charisma and adopt a transformational leadership style as means of motivating individuals and gaining their commitment.

It is of utmost importance to possess a comprehensive comprehension of both positive and negative emotions, as each category holds the potential to exert influence and sway individuals. Nevertheless, there exists a potential likelihood that positive emotions wield the greatest potency in this regard. If an individual possesses the ability to present happiness as an incentive, it promptly emerges as a more potent mechanism compared to employing sadness or fear as catalysts.

Managing Panic Attacks And Anxiety

Anxiety serves as a means for the body to signal that there is a need to attend to an aspect of oneself. As an illustration, my anxiety led me to perceive myself as a perfectionist, thereby impeding my progress. I possessed a strong drive for success; however, I perpetually experienced a sense of dissatisfaction with my accomplishments. I frequently undertook excessive responsibilities, thereby exerting additional strain on my mental and physical well-being. Furthermore, I possessed a strong inclination towards seeking approval from others, leading to the inevitable cultivation and exacerbation of anxiety within my existence.

Anxiety can be highly distressing and disorganized, however, upon recognizing the physical signs of unease, it becomes imperative to undertake a comprehensive process of restoration. It took me a number of years to develop the strategies that enabled me to manage my panic attacks and anxiety.

It is imperative to bear in mind that not all of these tips and techniques will yield the same results for every individual. That is attributed to our inherent individual differences. Nevertheless, although certain approaches may prove ineffective in your case, they will nonetheless stimulate and encourage you to devise your own strategies. Therefore, I would like to suggest a course of action to effectively manage your panic attacks and anxiety, while safeguarding your well-being and mental health.

Engage in critical analysis of your anxious cognitive tendencies.

You're not your thoughts. Acknowledge your cognitive tendencies towards anxiety, summon your bravery, and actively question and confront them. While it may appear alarming and implausible, employing this method can effectively eliminate detrimental thought patterns.

Whenever I experienced anxiety, I found myself plagued by physical discomfort and incessant envisioning of worst-case scenarios, beset by apprehension for impending circumstances. This tendency to engage in catastrophic thinking induced severe episodes of panic. I consistently experienced a sense of powerlessness and inadvertently perpetuated my tendencies towards anxious thought patterns instead of overcoming them.

When one finds oneself entertaining the belief that the most unfavorable outcome is looming, it is advisable to pose the question, "Is there any substantiated evidence supporting the likelihood of said outcome?" It is probable that the response would be in the negative. It is essential to recognize that all conceptualizations originate in the mind, including the formulation of worst-case scenarios. It is imperative that you address this issue and liberate your mind from such cognitive patterns.

In addition, individuals suffering from anxiety and panic attacks also experience various alternative cognitive patterns characterized by worry and apprehension:

Binary thinking - This is a cognitive tendency characterized by a challenge in perceiving shades of gray or finding a nuanced middle ground. As an example, should you harbor dissatisfaction towards your current employment and harbor intentions of resigning, it is imperative to acknowledge the simultaneous gratitude one should possess for this occupation, as it serves as a means to secure financial resources for sustenance and obligations. The majority of individuals possess such cognitive patterns, which serve as a hindrance in pursuing activities that bring them genuine enjoyment.

Making sweeping generalizations - This occurs when an individual concludes that a negative event is likely to recur simply because it has happened to them in the past. It bears resemblance to the apprehension regarding failure and can give rise to episodes of panic during pivotal occasions in one's life.

Divination - Your apprehensive mindset leads you to believe that you possess knowledge of forthcoming events in the immediate future. "I shall abstain from attempting as I am confident that it shall yield no success." It is commendable to rely on one's intuition, albeit caution must be exercised in relying on one's anxious thoughts.

Telepathy - You consistently presume to have an accurate understanding of the thoughts and perceptions others have towards you, whether they are acquaintances, colleagues, or even individuals with whom you have no prior relationship. Certainly, you seem to possess an extraordinary ability to read minds. Rest assured, the colleague whom you suspect has ill feelings towards you actually holds you in high regard.

The occurrence of incessant self-critical thoughts such as 'I lack intelligence,' 'My appearance is highly unattractive,' or 'I do not possess the necessary capabilities for that professional role' can potentially contribute to the development of significant anxiety disorders. Consequently, it is imperative to commence the process of eliminating such tendencies in order to alleviate the burden carried by your anxious mind.

You may be wondering, "How can I accomplish this?" I should clarify that it would be misleading to suggest that the process is simple. Managing negative thoughts requires a significant investment of time, self-discipline, and exertion. However, once you successfully break free from this detrimental thinking pattern, you will find it progressively easier to minimize the occurrence of your panic attacks.

Presented herewith are a number of pragmatic measures to extend assistance to you:

Identify and record all of your maladaptive cognitive patterns. Please provide personal illustrations for each pattern.

Now, I encourage you to embrace this challenge and transform those negative instances into positive ones. Take, for example, the statement, "I lack sufficient experience to be eligible for this position." This commonly uttered phrase encompasses various forms of negative thought patterns and can induce an anxious state that may culminate in a severe panic episode. Your mission at present is to fabricate an alternate phrasing with a more authentic and sanguine tone. Let us consider the following: 'Despite my limited experience in this field, I am confident in my ability to enhance it swiftly by obtaining this job.' Do you perceive the distinction between these statements? While the initial statement conveys a negative connotation, the subsequent sentence guarantees a pragmatic and favorable result.

Carefully review all the examples provided and identify any highly negative expressions you may have employed, such as "I can't do it." Substitute those with positive affirmations, such as "I will make an effort to accomplish it." It is conceivable that I may encounter failure, as it is a natural aspect of my humanity. Nevertheless, I view failure as an invaluable opportunity for growth and education."

In addition, it is possible to document your daily negative thoughts by jotting them down and alongside them, pen a more composed perspective.

The experience of a low mood is characterized by a negative emotional state, typically initiated by the manifestation of negative thought patterns. It is advisable to establish a connection between these two phenomena. If you happen to be experiencing melancholy, it is crucial to recognize the cognitive processes that have contributed to your current emotional state.

Upon acquiring the ability to attentively heed to your innermost thoughts, you shall come to acknowledge the predominantly pessimistic nature of your own mind. Your cognitive state is the primary catalyst for the manifestation of your anxiety and panic attacks.

Continuously strive to confront and overcome negative cognitive patterns in order to cultivate a mindset that is characterized by equality and positivity. Devote yourself daily to observing your thoughts meticulously, evaluating them critically, and exerting utmost effort to transform them.

Embrace your restless thoughts

Irrespective of the ailment, embracing it affords you an opportunity to be one stride nearer to recuperation. Acknowledge the state of anxiety that your mind is currently experiencing. Acknowledge the presence of panic attacks. Do not stifle these emotions, rather strive to comprehend them. Indeed, panic attacks engender a sense of apprehension, yet they do not impede the proper functioning of one's physiological responses.

Acceptance entails acknowledging that one is currently striving to overcome anxiety, and that despite undergoing the complete recovery process, feelings of anxiety and episodes of panic attacks may persist. Moreover, it entails acknowledging the possibility of a duration during which one's anxious thoughts persistently resurface. It is inherently common for individuals to experience occasional bouts of anxiety, as enduring a state of perpetual calmness is unattainable. Efficiently acquire the ability to embrace the situation, handle it proficiently, and progress forward.

Place yourself as a top priority.

Adequate rest, balanced nutrition, and regular exercise establish exceptional groundwork for effectively confronting anxiety and panic attacks. It is imperative to prioritize the well-being of both your physical and mental faculties in order to amass the necessary strength to confront your adversary, which in this case is anxiety.

Ensure that you find joy and amusement, establish a deep connection with your inner self, and employ a multitude of strategies to facilitate a sense of tranquility. Envelop yourself in the company of individuals who exhibit kindness and optimism, possessing positive outlooks. Practice self-compassion and refrain from harboring feelings of guilt due to experiencing anxiety.

Reconsider your lifestyle

Do you feel unhappy? Do you find yourself in a relationship that is characterized by toxicity? Are you inclined towards seeking approval and satisfying others? Are your friends real? Are you passionate about your profession? Take a moment to consider the message that your panic attacks are attempting to communicate, in order to effectively address the underlying issues within your life. Take the opportunity to reassess your lifestyle in order to ascertain the underlying causes of your anxiety.

Confront and conquer, instead of evading-

When confronted with anxiety, it is advisable not to refrain from engaging in activities that were previously pleasurable without confronting panic attacks. Regardless of the magnitude of distress or fear you may experience, persevere resolutely, assuring yourself that neither anxiety nor panic attacks pose any harm. The sense of anxiety will ultimately diminish as you confront and conquer it.

Begin perceiving each distressing circumstance as a minor obstacle that will ultimately result in a significant triumph." I am familiar with the experience of one's entire being, from the bones to the cells, compelling an individual to escape from a distressing circumstance. Nevertheless, it would be advantageous to refrain from indulging in anxious thoughts. Effortlessly navigate through the unpleasant emotions, recognizing that they will inevitably dissipate over time.

The act of evading engenders a cognitive association within your mind that involves apprehension, despite the absence of any actual grounds for concern. Enabling the persistence of anxiety is a consequence of avoidance. Exhibit the courage to confront and conquer it, rather than fostering its growth.

Do not let anxiety become an integral aspect of your existence.

It is quite alluring to disclose to others that you are experiencing feelings of anxiety, to share anxious content and images on your social media platforms, and to lament about the negative impact your anxious life and panic attacks have on your ability to achieve productivity and pursue your aspirations.

Engaging in discussions pertaining to anxiety, harboring concerns about it, and diligently observing its presence only serve to perpetuate and reinforce the restless state of your mind. Allow it to remain in its current state for the necessary duration, and it will naturally decrease in intensity.

Ensure that your daily regimen is well-organized, incorporating significant tasks and activities that engross your mind in more rewarding pursuits than anxiety.

Do not despair in your own abilities

Finally, believe in yourself. Bear in mind that your fortitude and strength are formidable, enabling you to overcome anxiety and panic episodes, much like numerous individuals have done in the past. Fortunately, anxiety does not equate to cancer and can be effectively addressed through non-invasive medical interventions.

Retain your belief in your ability to recover; perhaps not in the immediate future, but restoration is assured. In due time, you will come to perceive your anxiety as a divine boon, for it shall imbue you with heightened positivity, tremendous fortitude, and unparalleled compassion. Anxiety has the potential to instill in one the understanding of cherishing every invaluable moment and embracing life to its fullest extent.

Overcoming Shyness

Introverted individuals understand that the behaviors they develop are not merely a result of their reserve; rather, they approach life with a distinctive cognitive style compared to their more extroverted counterparts.

Children, just like adults, can experience the manifestations of severe shyness and social anxiety. Please be aware that numerous individuals with sociophobia have reported that their difficulties originated during their earlier years. Frequently, however, these issues might go unnoticed by educators, guidance counselors, mentors, and occasionally, even parents. This aims to provide a comprehensive discussion on the various manifestations of shyness issues in children, along with strategies for identifying them and determining the appropriate level of concern. In early childhood, timidity is commonly regarded as an endearing quality, exemplified by statements such as, "Observe her bashfulness; she seeks solace by burying her face in her mother's attire." Is that not endearing? When children are in the preschool stage, it is frequently observed that they display behaviors associated with shyness, including exhibiting stranger anxiety by engaging in actions such as hiding, crying, or seeking comfort from their mother when encountering a new individual. Additionally, they tend to remain exceptionally reticent in the presence of unfamiliar people or rely on their father for support in unfamiliar circumstances. Such behaviors, within reasonable expectations, can be considered typical for a child of preschool age. Nonetheless, they are quite atypical for a student in the fifth grade.

One of the challenges faced by parents is discerning the transition from what is considered typical behavior to behavior that is indicative of an underlying issue. What is deemed as developmentally suitable for a 3-year-old is seldom deemed as appropriate for an 11-year-old. However, given the intimate relationship parents share with their children and their prolonged observation of their development, parents frequently struggle to identify deviations in their children. It is common for parents to possess awareness of their children's high anxiety levels, yet they often tend to underestimate the extent of their children's anxiety in comparison to how the children perceive it themselves. What is the rationale behind this phenomenon? The reality is that our schedules are filled with obligations such as preparing meals and providing transportation, leaving us with limited awareness of our children's emotional experiences. We are discussing exceptional parents, not those who are inadequate. Emotions are experienced with intensity, yet they are subjective in nature: without verbal communication, discerning someone's anxiety or discomfort can prove to be quite challenging. Occasionally, children may communicate with us, although they may lack the appropriate vocabulary to express themselves coherently to adults. Adolescents, undoubtedly, exhibit a predilection for withholding information from us.

In younger children, specifically those under the age of 8 or 9, it is more common for them to articulate their physical symptoms rather than expressly communicate their feelings of anxiety or fear. The following outlines several physical symptoms commonly observed in socially anxious children:

> Abdominal discomforts

> Nausea or an uncomfortable sensation in the abdominal area

> Nausea

> Elevated heart rate

> Dyspnea

> Dizziness

> Xerostomia

> Blushing

> Headaches

If your child articulates these symptoms within the context of social situations, it is possible that they are experiencing social anxiety. For instance, in the event that your son expresses discomfort in his abdominal region prior to attending school in the morning, one plausible explanation, among potentially other factors, could be social anxiety. Alternatively, if a child expresses feelings of dizziness in anticipation of giving an oral presentation in the classroom, it would be prudent for the teacher to consider the possibility of underlying social anxiety.

Are there alternative methods of identifying if your child is experiencing symptoms of anxiety? Indeed, one can frequently deduce from individuals' conduct that they are experiencing feelings of anxiety, unease, or distress. When it comes to social anxiety, valuable insights can be gained by observing the patterns of avoidance exhibited by your child. What types of circumstances do children with social anxiety typically attempt to evade?

> Verbalizing during class discussions

> Delivering oral presentations

> Oral reading

> Engaging in examination

"> Displaying information on the whiteboard

> Consuming food in the presence of others.

> Extending an invitation for children to join in recreational activities

> Attending social gatherings

> Playing sports

If your child demonstrates a tendency to evade or elude engagement in such activities, it is possible that he or she is grappling with social anxiety. What is the basis for your certainty? Commence by inquiring with your child, "I have observed that you have displayed reluctance towards attending certain birthday gatherings for your classmates." The social gatherings appear to be quite enjoyable. Could you please provide an explanation for your reluctance to attend? Do you have any concerns or anxieties? In some instances, children may experience apprehension concerning appearing foolish, expressing themselves inadequately, or garnering disapproval from their peers. Do any of these concerns cause you uneasiness? Additionally, you can engage in conversation with your child's teacher to acquire insights into their participation in group activities, verbal contributions in class, and similar aspects.

Selective Mutism

Selective Mutism is a type of social anxiety disorder that impacts certain young children. While it is indeed typical for a 4- or 5-year-old child to exhibit hesitancy in expressing themselves in front of unfamiliar individuals, especially adults, it is concerning and detrimental for a child to remain completely silent for an extended duration. This statement does not pertain to children who are experiencing delays in their speech or language development. We are pertaining to youngsters who exhibit proficient verbal skills within the presence of their parents, siblings, and perhaps a select few confidants, yet remain reticent in the company of others. When this phenomenon takes place, it is referred to as selective Mutism.

How to Engage in Conversations with Unfamiliar Individuals

Frequently, as adults, we exhibit a reluctance to engage in conversation with individuals whom we have not previously acquainted ourselves with. We may avert our gaze to avoid interaction. We may feign obliviousness to individuals. We may potentially detach ourselves from them.

Engaging in conversation with individuals whom we are unfamiliar with can be particularly challenging, especially for those who speak English as a second language. You might be self-conscious. You may encounter difficulties in determining the precise word that you seek. You may find yourself at a loss for words. You may perceive your English language proficiency to be insufficient. It is possible that you may perceive yourself to have experienced a failure.

Engaging in conversation with unfamiliar individuals can be an anxiety-inducing experience for the majority of individuals, regardless of possessing considerable charm and self-assurance.

What is the primary method to utilize? Questions. As long as the other individual is speaking, it is unnecessary for you to express anything beyond acknowledgement through phrases such as "mhmm," "tell me more," and "interesting."

That is considerably more effortless compared to endeavoring to engage them through one's anecdotes.

Do not merely inquire about a single matter and proceed without further exploration. After the interlocutor has concluded their response, proceed to inquire further by posing a supplementary question. This assists in reducing the possibility of appearing as though you are conducting an interrogation or an interview.

As an example, in the event that you inquire, "From which location do you originate?" and they respond by stating, "Minnesota," you may proceed to ask, "What prompted your relocation?", "Which notable resemblances exist between Minnesota and our current location?", "If given the choice, who would you have brought with you from Minnesota?", "What are your preferred destinations within Minnesota?", or "What are the must-see attractions I should not overlook when visiting Minnesota?" or any other question centered around Minnesota.

When initially initiating the conversation, one possesses limited knowledge about the individual in question.

Prioritize the initiation of a discourse as the foremost task. There are numerous methodologies available to accomplish this task, and I strongly encourage you to engage in exploration and experimentation. Initially, it is possible to remark upon a shared aspect, commencing with the traditional and well-known topic of weather. Additionally, one may engage in conversation regarding the mutual geographic setting or a subject of mutual visual interest. While this may appear to be a trivial matter, it is imperative to establish a preliminary connection before embarking on more captivating subjects.

A viable alternative would be to commence with a flattering remark. The act of bestowing compliments is enjoyable, and it holds even greater delight to receive them, particularly when they originate from an unfamiliar individual. It is often more plausible to accept compliments from individuals who possess limited familiarity with oneself.

Getting Through

Now that the discourse has commenced, allow me to provide a few guidelines on maintaining its seamless progression. Provide input on shared interests and employ attentive perception and inquisitiveness. Irrespective individuals tend to appreciate it when further inquiries are posed. It exemplifies your attentiveness, as opposed to contemplation of a response.

One possibility could be: "It is worth contemplating the act of revealing a personal aspect about oneself, as it fosters a sense of trust and fosters a reciprocal attitude."

I initiated a conversation with a woman by inquiring about the progress of her day. She provided an ambiguous reply, leading me to suspect that the exchange could potentially be concluded. Subsequently, she inquired about the same matter, to which I responded that I had embarked on an extraordinary expedition. Subsequently, she disclosed to me that she had recently become aware of her pregnancy. Despite this, she intended to return to work and maintain a façade of normalcy, as she prioritized informing her loved ones before making any public announcements. Nonetheless, she experienced a sense of security when confiding in someone completely unknown to her, with whom she would never cross paths again. I was deeply privileged.

Lastly, maintaining patience is of utmost importance. Engaging in conversations with individuals may result in their surprise, requiring some time for them to adapt to the notion that your relationship is solely founded on friendship. Continue persevering, and for the majority of instances, you will succeed in finding your rhythm.

Body Language And How You Appear

In the context of an interview, one's appearance holds significance in the perception of the interviewer. Regardless of the outcome, our appearance has an impact on the opinion formed by the interviewer. Should we opt to leave an unprofessional impression, it is likely to be the lasting perception they hold. Nevertheless, should we dedicate ourselves to enhancing our outward image, we will undoubtedly establish a compelling initial perception. It is imperative to uphold equilibrium and possess discernment regarding righteousness. It poses a challenge to reach that location upon initial observation. Nevertheless, it is imperative that we exert our utmost effort in this regard, and we can effectively accomplish this by paying close attention to our attire, diligently maintaining our grooming standards, and skillfully managing our hairstyle, as these aspects will undeniably make a lasting impression during an interview.

Appropriate attire for the occasion

Typically, the majority of interviews will necessitate the donning of conservative attire. Typically, this entails wearing a formal shirt, tie, and trousers for men, and dress trousers paired with a blouse, a dress, or a blouse and skirt for women, in most cases. It is imperative that you adhere to the regulations governing overall appearance in the establishment of your desired employment. If the individuals featured in a promotional campaign are depicted donning formal attire such as a suit and tie, it is advisable to follow suit and dress accordingly. It will facilitate distinguishing yourself and demonstrate a high level of commitment towards the interview procedure.

Women should refrain from wearing any attire that causes undue discomfort, including but not limited to high-heeled shoes and other similar items. It is imperative to maximize one's comfort to the greatest extent possible. It would be undesirable to appear as though you disembarked from an aircraft and perspired profusely due to excessive layering of garments. Consequently, you aspire to present yourself in a polished manner, while maintaining optimal levels of comfort.

It is advised that individuals of all genders refrain from wearing attire that will excessively attract attention to themselves. This encompasses ostentatious, vintage, or vividly colored attire, which would be perceived unfavorably during the interview. Keep in mind the imperative of establishing a positive impact, thus it would be advisable for you to adhere to attire that is both comfortable and comprised of earth tones or dark hues, as such choices will prevent you from drawing excessive attention or appearing flushed.

Body art

Tattoos have become increasingly popular among contemporary individuals. They are progressively gaining greater levels of acceptance. Nevertheless, when it comes to professional environments, it is generally more advisable to conceal tattoos instead of openly displaying them, especially within conservative corporate settings where their visibility may be disapproved of. It is advisable to prioritize safety over regret. Tattoos may elicit an adverse initial impression from individuals harboring biased attitudes towards them.

Jewelry worn on the ears and nose

A significant number of individuals opt to adorn themselves with earrings and nose rings. For women, it is appropriate to adorn oneself with a small, understated pair of earrings. Nevertheless, the use of nose rings is highly discouraged. It is advisable for individuals to abstain from wearing nose rings to job interviews, regardless of the location or company. Men have the option to wear earrings. Nevertheless, it is advisable to refrain from engaging in such forms of expression, particularly when interacting with more traditional supervisors or executives who may disapprove of such behavior.

Personal hygiene and appearance maintenance

For women, it would be customary for them to exhibit good personal grooming and maintain their hair in a manner that is tidy and well-kept. Men are expected to maintain a well-groomed appearance, which includes being free of facial hair and styling their hair in a tidy and presentable manner. It is crucial to present oneself in the best possible manner during the interview, exhibiting meticulous effort in crafting one's appearance for this occasion. Furthermore, it is advisable to perform oral hygiene practices such as brushing your teeth and using dental floss on the day of the interview to ensure the absence of any debris in your teeth before entering the premises.

www.ingramcontent.com/pod-product-compliance
Lightning Source LLC
Chambersburg PA
CBHW050027130526
44590CB00042B/2035